BUMST

This Book Belongs To
Sophia
& Natalie
(404) 388-9511

Glumby
the
Grumbler

A Beastie Book About
Being Grateful

Glumby
the
Grumbler

A Beastie Book About
Being Grateful

Written By
Ron Berry
Bartholomew
Patricia and Frederick McKissack

Illustrated By
Bartholomew

Consultants: Stephen W. Garber, Ph.D.
                    Marianne Daniels Garber, Ph.D.
                    Robyn Freedman Spizman

Managing Editor: Doug Boggs
Layout Design: Steve Sheldon
Typography: Borst Designs
Cover Design: Paul Lewis
Coloring Artists: Donna Baker
                    Gary Currant

ISBN 1-883761-00-X

Looks like another terrible day!

Glumby is a complaining Beastie.

When things go wrong, she complains.

Nothing **ever** goes right!

Moaner Liza

4

When things go right, she complains.

I don't like that kind!

My eat!

5

BBBRRING

Complaint list
Newspaper in bushes
Milkman too noisy!

The alarm clock rings. Brrrrring!

6

"Oh, oh, oh. It's too early to get up," Glumby moans.

7

Glumby gets ready for school.
"I don't like blue. This sweater
itches. My socks don't fit. I
don't have anything to wear."

8

"Oh, oh, oh. This is going to be a terrible day!" What could Glumby do to get off to a better start?

9

The Squeeky wheel gets the GREASE!

Where is my potholder?

"To DO" Complain to neighbor just because!

This pancake is tough!

There are pancakes for breakfast. They smell so good.

"I don't want pancakes I want cereal," Glumby grumbles. What should Glumby have said instead?

11

Glumby never has anything
nice to say about anyone...

It's too crowded!

It's too bumpy!

Sigh.

Beastiville School

STOP!

...and she finds fault with everything.

13

This isn't the grade I wanted!

You never went over that in class.

There were too many problems.

Stupid test!

Even when Glumby goes to school, she does nothing but complain: She missed a problem on her math test...

14

Suppose we give you an A, shorten your class periods, have longer recesses. Would that make you happy?

Well... it's a start!

PRINCIPAL

Time
Recess
Lunch
Students
desk
books
Math
playground
teachers
more on back

...Recess isn't long enough...
Her classes are too boring.

15

At lunchtime, Glumby bothers everyone with her grumblings.

16

Why do you think Glumby is sitting by herself?

It's too cold.

It's too deep.

Is there toxic waste?

Something bit me!

LIFE GUARD

Glumby never has fun going anywhere because she's so busy complaining...

18

sand 50¢ rental

Eats!

HOO-BOY!

Surf's up?

HANG SIX

IOMP!

Sun Sun Sun

...complaining... complaining.

19

This rain is too wet!

Glumby complains if it rains.

ICK!

The sun is too hot!

She complains when it's sunny.

Glumby is always bored too. "There's nothing to do," she grumbles.

22

Tag, you're it!

Oh, Brother!

TOYS

Beastie Land

What could Glumby do to not be so bored?

23

Everybody take just one.

I just baked these.

I get the biggest!

I don't like rutabaga cookie

Glumby complains all day long. Her favorite words are, "Oh, oh, oh! I don't like..."

24

What a complainer. I'm telling!

Too slow!

Too high!

What would you like to say to Glumby?

25

Glumby gets ready for bed.
"What an awful day," she says.

26

27

Glumby is a complaining Beastie.

It's too quiet!

I can't sleep when the moon's out.

The Little Train that Couldn't

She complains all the time.
What about you?

29

It's too hot to dress that way.

But I...

Huh?

Remember:

- No one likes to be around someone who is always complaining.
- Complaining never makes anything better.

That's a dumb bike.

Ack!

If you want to be more positive and enjoy the things around you, do these things:

31

These flowers are pretty.

BG BEASTIE GARDEN

It smells.

Isn't this nice?

It's too hot.

- Focus on the good things around you instead of the bad.

32

The Gizzard Gumbo is Outstanding.

Excellent!

The Crabapple stew is good too.

These are not my favorite.

- Be thankful for what you have rather than complain about what you don't have.

33

You sure dress weird.

I heard you got an "A" in Math.

- If you cannot say something nice about someone, don't say anything at all.

I don't like these rules.

The ball is too old.

This is a fun game.

It sure is!

It's better than chasing mice.

- Don't find fault with everything. Look for the positive side.

35

Doesn't anything work around here?

UGH!

Dumb school!

- If things need changing, don't just complain.

Maybe the janitor could fix the swing.

Good idea!

• Make helpful suggestions.

37

Zonk the destructive

Crassy the crude

How many of these beasties can you find in this book?

Twitte the tattletal

38

You can't go swimming right after you ate!

Gorger the greedy

Bertha the bossy

Belch!

This water's cold. I'm telling!

Dingy the dirty

39